Fire Fight! THE BRAVEST

Hotshots

by Meish Goldish

Consultant: Dan Mallia, Superintendent
Redding Interagency Hotshot Crew
Redding, California

BEARPORT
PUBLISHING

New York, New York

Credits

Cover and Title Page, © ZUMA Press, Inc./Alamy and © USDA Photo/Alamy; 4–5, © Brian Kliesen/USDA Forest Service; 5T, © John Fowler; 5B, © Kari Greer Photography; 6–7, © Kari Greer Photography; 8, © USDA Photo/Alamy; 8B, © Public Domain; 9, © Marcio Jose Sanchez/Associated Press; 10–11, © Zuma Press Inc./Alamy; 12, © USDA; 13, © Craig Allyn Rose/San José Fire Department Photographer; 14, © Zuma Press Inc./Alamy; 15T, © lasconfirechas3/Public Domain; 15B, © Reuters/Corbis; 16, © Idaho Stateman/Getty Images; 17T, © Kari Greer Photography; 17B, © smikeymikey1/Shutterstock; 18, © Kari Greer Photography; 19, © Visions of America/Superstock; 20, © Zuma Press Inc./Alamy; 21, © Kari Greer Photography; 22, © Kari Greer Photography; 23, © Jim Peaco; 24, © Joshua Lott/Corbis; 25, © Julie Jacobson/Associated Press; 26, © Kari Greer Photography; 27, © Kari Greer Photography; 28TL, © Kari Greer Photography; 28TR, © photka/Shutterstock; 28BL, © Hustvedt/Wikipedia Creative Commons; 28BR, © Public Domain; 29T, © Ambient Images Inc/Superstock; 29BL, © Zuma Press Inc./Alamy; 29BR, © Nito/Shutterstock; 31, © USDA Photo/Alamy.

Publisher: Kenn Goin
Senior Editor: Joyce Tavolacci
Creative Director: Spencer Brinker
Design: Emma Randall
Photo Researcher: Ruby Tuesday Books

> **This book is dedicated to the 19 brave hotshots who lost their lives while battling a wildfire near Yarnell, Arizona, in 2013.**

Library of Congress Cataloging-in-Publication Data

Goldish, Meish.
 Hotshots / by Meish Goldish ; consultant, Dan Mallia, Superintendent Redding Interagency Hotshot Crew, Redding, California.
     pages cm. — (Fire fight! The bravest)
 Includes bibliographical references and index.
 ISBN 978-1-62724-099-4 (library binding) — ISBN 1-62724-099-3 (library binding)
 1. Fire fighters—Juvenile literature. I. Title.
 HD8039.F5G653 2014
 634.9'618—dc23
                        2013035389

For more information, write to Bearport Publishing Company, Inc., 45 West 21st Street, Suite 3B, New York, New York 10010. Printed in the United States of America.

10 9 8 7 6 5 4 3 2 1

Contents

Forest on Fire!

June 26, 2011, was a hot, windy day in New Mexico's Santa Fe National Forest. As the wind blew through the forest, a tree fell and knocked down a **power line**. Sparks from the electrical wire set fire to grasses and other plants on the ground. In no time, the dry forest began to burn as high winds quickly spread the flames.

The wildfire in the Santa Fe National Forest spread quickly because little rain had fallen in months. As a result, the grasses and trees were very dry.

Every minute, the blaze burned 60 acres (24 hectares)—about the size of 45 football fields! By the time help arrived, thousands of acres of forestland were lit up by bright orange flames. The giant **wildfire** was much too large for firefighters to **extinguish** with water hoses. This was a job for a special group of firefighters called hotshots!

A gigantic tower of smoke from the forest fire could be seen from miles away.

Hotshots are firefighters who are specially trained to battle forest fires and other large wildfires. They often work in teams of 20 members.

5

A Huge Job

As the huge fire in the Santa Fe National Forest raged on, several teams of hotshots arrived to battle the blaze. They traveled from nearby states to fight the wildfire. One team, the Vale Hotshots, flew from their home base in Oregon. After landing in New Mexico, the team raced to the site of the fire.

Vale hotshots from Oregon get ready to battle the blazing wildfire.

A team of hotshots marches toward the smoky wildfire in the Santa Fe National Forest.

The hotshots had a tough job ahead. The forest was extremely hot and smoky. In half a day, the fire had burned 43,000 acres (17,401 hectares) and was still moving fast. Crews needed to work quickly to stop the blaze, but how would they get the fire under control?

CANADA

UNITED STATES

MEXICO

N
W E
S

Colorado

Santa Fe
National Forest

New Mexico

Texas

There are about 110 hotshot teams in the United States. Most are based in western states, where wildfires occur more frequently.

Tools of the Trade

To battle the wildfire in the Santa Fe National Forest, the hotshots carried special equipment in large backpacks. They brought shovels, rakes, and **chain saws**. Each team member also had a special tool called a **Pulaski**—a combination ax and hoe. How do these tools help hotshots fight a wildfire?

Working close to a wildfire, hotshots feel the intense heat of its flames.

The Pulaski was named for Ed Pulaski, a forest ranger who invented the tool in 1911. It can be used to dig in soil and chop wood.

Hotshots use their tools to dig a path called a **firebreak** around the spreading blaze. With shovels and rakes, teams clear away all burnable material—including branches, leaves, and grasses—from the path. When the wildfire reaches the firebreak, the flames have nothing to burn in the empty path. The fire is starved of its **fuel** and dies out.

Hotshots create a firebreak, which is usually about 3 to 10 feet (0.9 to 3 m) wide.

Large wildfires are too big to be extinguished with water hoses. Instead, hotshots contain the wildfire by circling it with a firebreak and then letting the fire burn out on its own.

Race Against Time

To stop a wildfire from spreading, a team of hotshots must work quickly to dig a firebreak. Every member has a specific job to do. Some hotshots cut down trees and saw logs that lie in the fire's path. Others chop **brush** and branches. Still others clear away the material that's been cut along the path. Together, the hotshots "act like a machine," says Frank Carroll, a former hotshot.

Hotshots use chain saws to cut down trees in order to create a wide, empty path around the fire.

In one hour, a team of hotshots can dig a firebreak that is about 400 feet (122 m) long. That's about the length of a football field.

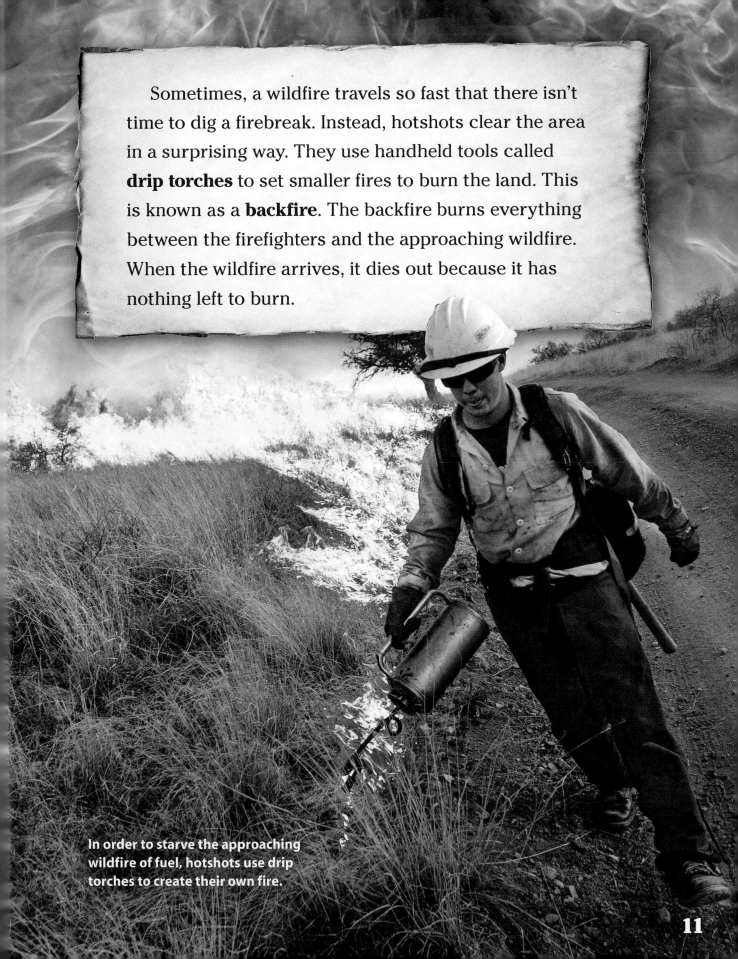

Sometimes, a wildfire travels so fast that there isn't time to dig a firebreak. Instead, hotshots clear the area in a surprising way. They use handheld tools called **drip torches** to set smaller fires to burn the land. This is known as a **backfire**. The backfire burns everything between the firefighters and the approaching wildfire. When the wildfire arrives, it dies out because it has nothing left to burn.

In order to starve the approaching wildfire of fuel, hotshots use drip torches to create their own fire.

In Case of Emergency

Hotshots never know when a fire is going to change direction. A shift in wind may suddenly send a wildfire or backfire rushing straight toward them. When that happens, the hotshots race to a planned **safety zone**. Often it's an area that has already burned so that the approaching flames can't spread there.

Hotshots moving away from a fire to a safe area

Sometimes, however, the safety zone is too far away to reach in time. Then the hotshots have one final option. Each of them carries a lightweight tent folded in their backpack. The tent can stand up to heat that is about 1,000°F (538°C). In an instant, they can open the tent and take cover inside. The tent can protect a hotshot for about two minutes, which might be enough time for the fire to pass, leaving the person inside unharmed.

A fire safety tent is made of **aluminum** and **fiberglass**.

A fire safety tent

Dirty Work

Hotshot teams often work 12 to 18 hours a day in areas that are hot, dusty, and smoky. To protect their bodies, they wear hard hats, long-sleeved shirts, long pants, and thick boots. They do this in extreme heat while carrying 45 pounds (20 kg) of gear or more as they clear the land.

Hotshots work in dirty conditions and in temperatures that often rise well above 100°F (38°C).

"It's the worst yard work you've ever done, all day, times a thousand," said hotshot Eric Neitzel. At night, hotshots sleep outside on the ground in their fire clothing. "No showers for weeks, very little change of clothes," said Eric. Plus, there's dirt everywhere. "You've got dirt in your nails, dirt in your ears, down your shirt."

A hotshot team getting a meal after a long day

Hotshots may work up to 30 days in a row without a day off. Then they get a few days to rest before returning to the job.

Hotshots taking a break

Getting Help

Hotshots work hard to contain a wildfire. Yet they usually don't battle the blaze all by themselves. If the fire is in a remote area with few or no roads, **smokejumpers** often **parachute** to the site before the hotshots arrive. They work to contain the fire using the same kinds of tools that the hotshots use.

A smokejumper leaps from an airplane.

Hotshots receive other help as well. **Tanker planes** fly overhead and drop **fire-retardant** chemicals onto the flames. The wet, sticky chemicals cool trees and other plants so they burn more slowly or not at all. Helicopters carry huge buckets of water that are dumped onto the fire. If there are roads nearby, fire engines may arrive to spray water on parts of the blaze.

A tanker dropping fire retardant onto a wildfire

Water being released on part of a wildfire

Fire-retardant chemicals dropped on a wildfire are brightly colored, so pilots can see which parts of the fire site have been treated.

Finishing the Job

Even after hotshots put out the fire, there is more work to be done. The hotshots must check the ground and "mop up." They walk slowly across the burned land and carefully feel it with their hands. Why?

Hotshots use their bare hands to check the ground for heat.

As they cross the land, the hotshots search for "hot spots." These are patches of land where the fire is still **smoldering**. Each hot spot must be put out entirely so the fire does not restart later. When they are finally done, the hotshots head home.

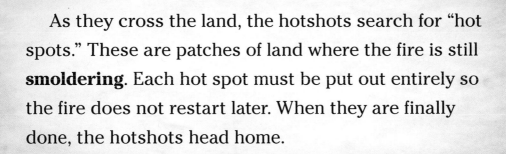
It took hotshots nearly six weeks to contain the wildfire that began in June 2011 in the Santa Fe National Forest. The fire burned over 156,000 acres (63,131 hectares) of land.

Hotshots marching home after battling a fierce blaze

Passing the Test

A lot of hard work and training is involved in becoming a hotshot. Matt Prentiss is a member of the Wyoming Hotshots. Part of Matt's job is to get hotshot **trainees** in shape so they're ready to walk long distances with heavy gear—and, ultimately, battle fires in the wilderness.

A hotshot uses a Pulaski to remove brush while carrying heavy gear.

 Most of the people who become hotshots are already trained as firefighters.

Matt puts his **recruits** through a series of tough physical tests. They start by hiking up and down steep hills for several hours. Trainees must also do 40 sit-ups and 25 push-ups in 2 minutes. Then they run 1.5 (2.4 km) miles in under 11 minutes.

The final challenge for hotshot trainees is the "pack test." While wearing 45 pounds (20 kg) of gear, the hotshots must hike 3 miles (4.8 km) in just 45 minutes.

Understanding Wildfires

Hotshots need more than just physical strength, however. They must also become wildfire experts. For example, trainees learn that a forest fire usually travels less than 9 miles per hour (14 kmh) on flat land. Yet a fire burning up a steep, tree-lined slope moves two to three times faster.

A raging wildfire races up a steep slope

Hotshots also learn how weather affects a wildfire's course. For example, wind can easily change the speed and direction of roaring flames. Giant wildfires called **firestorms** suck in air and create their own high winds. Those winds may blow **embers** several miles away, starting new fires. Hotshots must know all this—and more—before they battle a blaze.

A firestorm

A fire needs three things in order to burn: heat, **oxygen**, and any burnable material in its path. Hotshots know that they can stop a wildfire by taking away its fuel.

Deadly Risks

Even with all their training, hotshots still face great danger on the job. In June 2013, the Granite Mountain Hotshots were battling a raging wildfire near the town of Yarnell, Arizona. On the third day of the blaze, the wind suddenly shifted. It sent a wall of flames straight toward the hotshot crew.

The fire near Yarnell, Arizona, burned hundreds of trees.

Nineteen of the twenty team members took cover under their safety tents. However, the shelters couldn't stand up to the extreme temperature of the fire. All 19 hotshots lost their lives. It was one of the worst firefighting tragedies in U.S. history. President Barack Obama praised the hotshots as "heroes . . . who **selflessly** put themselves in harm's way" to protect others.

Photos of the 19 fallen Granite Mountain Hotshot firefighters and the lone survivor (right) of the fatal blaze hang on the fence outside Fire Station No. 7 in Prescott, Arizona.

The twentieth member of the Granite Mountain Hotshots was moving the team's truck at the time the flames struck. He escaped the blaze.

Why Be a Hotshot?

Luckily, tragedies like the one in Yarnell, Arizona, are rare. Yet with such danger on the job, why would anyone wish to be a hotshot? Brandon Hess, a hotshot based in South Dakota, explains, "I love the outdoors, and I love feeling that I have a part in protecting the public lands."

Hotshots risk their lives to protect both property and people.

There are about 2,200 hotshots in the United States. Most are men between 25 and 35 years old. However, some women also work as hotshots.

Patrick Moore, a hotshot in Arizona, believes strongly in the hotshots' motto: Safety. Teamwork. **Professionalism**. "When you become a hotshot, it becomes a part of you," he says. "It isn't just a job." With dedicated fighters like these, hotshots will continue their heroic work, bravely battling deadly wildfires.

By battling forest fires, hotshots help save America's forests.

Hotshots' Gear

Hotshots use many types of equipment to make a firebreak or set a backfire.

A *chain saw* is used to cut down trees and saw logs in the path of a firebreak.

A *shovel* is used to remove dirt from a firebreak.

A *rake* loosens and scrapes away small rocks, twigs, and dirt from a firebreak.

A *drip torch* shoots flames on the ground in order to set a backfire.

A *Pulaski* has two main parts—an ax and a hoe.

The ax is used to chop brush and branches from a firebreak.

The *hoe* is used to loosen and dig dirt.

Hotshots wear special gear to protect them on the job.
Here is some of their gear.

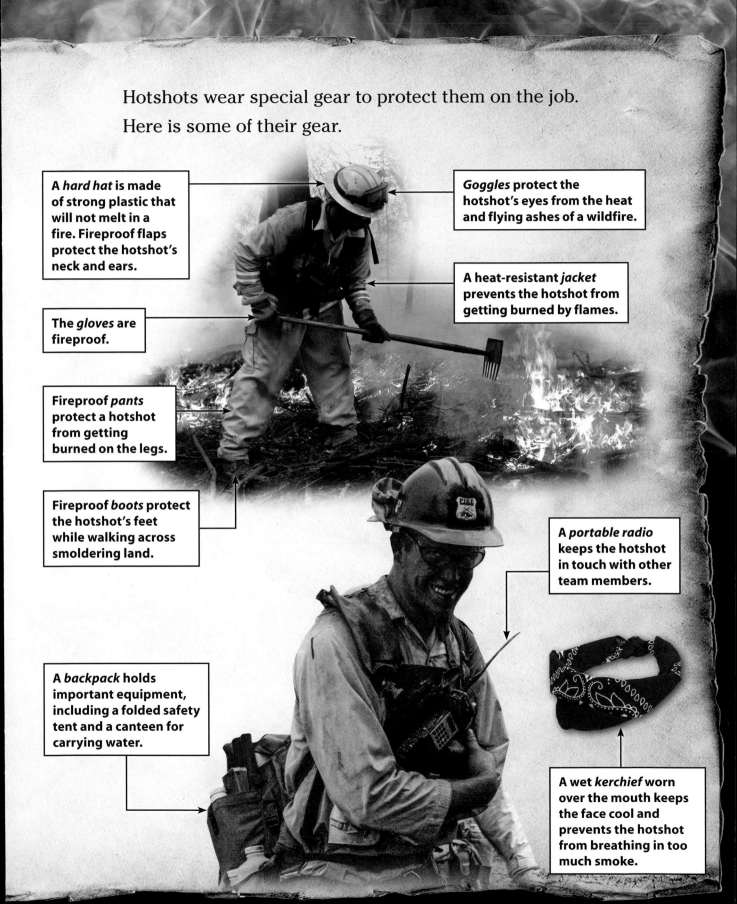

A *hard hat* is made of strong plastic that will not melt in a fire. Fireproof flaps protect the hotshot's neck and ears.

Goggles protect the hotshot's eyes from the heat and flying ashes of a wildfire.

A heat-resistant *jacket* prevents the hotshot from getting burned by flames.

The *gloves* are fireproof.

Fireproof *pants* protect a hotshot from getting burned on the legs.

Fireproof *boots* protect the hotshot's feet while walking across smoldering land.

A *portable radio* keeps the hotshot in touch with other team members.

A *backpack* holds important equipment, including a folded safety tent and a canteen for carrying water.

A wet *kerchief* worn over the mouth keeps the face cool and prevents the hotshot from breathing in too much smoke.

Glossary

aluminum (uh-LOO-muh-nuhm) a light, silver-colored metal that resists heat and flames

backfire (BAK-fire) a fire started on purpose to stop an advancing wildfire

brush (BRUHSH) a thick growth of small trees, bushes, and shrubs

chain saws (CHAYN sawz) gasoline-powered saws that have chains with cutting teeth

drip torches (DRIP TORCH-iz) small, hand-held torches that shoot flames in order to start fires

embers (EM-burz) the hot, glowing remains of a fire

extinguish (ek-STING-wish) to put out a fire

fiberglass (FYE-bur-glass) a strong material made from fine threads of glass

firebreak (FIRE-brayk) a path cleared around a forest fire to stop flames from spreading

fire-retardant (*fire*-ri-TARD-uhnt) something that slows down the speed with which something burns

firestorms (FIRE-stormz) huge fires that push air and create their own strong winds

fuel (FYOO-uhl) something that is burned, such as wood, to produce heat or power

oxygen (OK-suh-juhn) a colorless, odorless gas in the air that people breathe and that helps fires burn

parachute (PA-ruh-*shoot*) to jump out of a plane or helicopter using a cloth covering attached to ropes that slows the fall

power line (POU-ur LINE) a wire that carries electricity

professionalism (pruh-FESH-uh-nuhl-*iz*-uhm) the skill expected of someone working in a particular job

Pulaski (puh-LASS-kee) a firefighting tool that works as both an ax and a hoe

recruits (ri-KROOTS) individuals who have recently joined a group or organization

safety zone (SAYF-tee ZOHN) a place where firefighters can move to if a fire gets too close

selflessly (SELF-liss-lee) showing more concern for the needs of others than for oneself

smokejumpers (SMOHK-juhmp-urz) firefighters who parachute into a forest to battle a blaze

smoldering (SMOHL-dur-ing) smoking and burning slowly with no flames

tanker planes (TANG-kur PLAYNZ) airplanes that drop chemicals on a wildfire in order to put it out

trainees (tray-NEEZ) people who are being taught how to perform a new job

wildfire (WILDE-fire) a large, out-of-control fire, often in a wooded area

Bibliography

Beil, Karen Magnuson. *Fire in Their Eyes: Wildfires and the People Who Fight Them.* San Diego, CA: Harcourt (1999).

Krauss, Erich. *Wall of Flame: The Heroic Battle to Save Southern California.* Hoboken, NJ: Wiley (2006).

Read More

Costain, Meredith. *Devouring Flames: The Story of Forest Fires.* Washington, D.C.: National Geographic (2006).

Morrison, Taylor. *Wildfire.* Boston: Houghton Mifflin (2006).

Thomas, William David. *Forest Firefighter (Cool Careers: Adventure).* Pleasantville, NY: Gareth Stevens (2008).

Learn More Online

To learn more about hotshots, visit
www.bearportpublishing.com/FireFight

Index

About the Author

Meish Goldish has written more than 200 books for children.
His book *Disabled Dogs* was a Junior Library Guild Selection in 2013.
He lives in Brooklyn, New York.